William Shakespeare's

Henry V

EDITED BY
Philip Page and Marilyn Pettit

ILLUSTRATED BY
Philip Page

Published in association with

Hodder & Stoughton

A MEMBER OF THE HODDER HEADLINE GROUP

Orders: please contact Bookpoint Ltd, 130 Milton Park, Abingdon, Oxon OX14 4SB.
Telephone: (44) 01235 827720, Fax: (44) 01235 400454. Lines are open from 9.00–6.00,
Monday to Saturday, with a 24 hour message answering service. Email address:
orders@bookpoint.co.uk

British Library Cataloguing in Publication Data
A catalogue record for this tile is available from The British Library

ISBN 0 340 77473 8

First published 2000
Impression number   10 9 8 7 6 5 4 3 2
Year   2005 2004 2003 2002

Cover illustration Lee Stinton
Typeset by Fakenham Photosetting Ltd, Fakenham, Norfolk NR21 8NN
Printed in Great Britain for Hodder & Stoughton Educational, a division of Hodder
Headline Plc, 338 Euston Road, London 3BH by J. W. Arrowsmith Ltd, Bristol

Contents

About the play

King Henry V is one of Shakespeare's historical plays. It is based on real events, and tells the story of how King Henry of England fought a war against France and won!

Shakespeare read what other people had written about this war and using this information, or sources, he wrote his play.

He changed some of the facts and added new characters to the action, because he wanted to write a play that would make the audience feel proud of England, and one that would also entertain them.

He liked to make his audience laugh as well as think seriously about events, so he had comical characters who could also be fierce.

Reading or watching this play still makes us think about serious things, like war and the way kings and common people behave.

Read on ... and see if you can spot the comic characters. See what you think about war once you have finished your reading.

Cast of characters

King Henry V

Exeter   **Westmorland**   **Salisbury**

English nobles and officers in King Henry's army.

Fluellen   **Gower**   **Williams**   **Bates**

A Welsh   An English   Soldiers in King Henry's army.

captain.   captain.

Scroop   Cambridge   Grey

Three traitors who plan to kill King Henry.

Charles VI
The French King.

Isabel
The French Queen.

Princess Katherine
Their daughter.

The Dauphin
Eldest son of the
French King.

Orleans

Constable
French noblemen.

Rambures

Burgundy
A duke who helps to make peace
between France and England.

Montjoy
The French herald
(messenger).

Alice
Katherine's servant.

Pistol
A small-time
villain who joins
Henry's army.

Hostess
Pistol's wife.

Bardolph

Nym

The Boy

Pistol's comrades who get killed in France.

vi

Can this **cockpit** hold
The **vasty** fields of France? Or may we cram
Within this **wooden O** the very **casques**
That did **affright** the air at Agincourt?

Let us on your imaginary forces work.
Suppose within the girdle of these walls
Are now confined two mighty monarchies,
Whose **high upreared and abutting fronts**
The perilous narrow ocean parts asunder.

'Tis your thoughts that now must deck our kings,
Carry them here and there, jumping o'er times,
Turning th'accomplishment of many years
Into an hour-glass.

Admit me Chorus to this history,
Who prologue-like your humble patience pray,
Gently to hear, kindly to judge our play.

cockpit & wooden O – the theatre   **vasty** – vast or wide   **casques** – helmets   **affright** – frighten
high ... asunder – the cliffs of France and England, separated by the Channel.

Think about it

What words tell you that Shakespeare's theatre had very few props?

Act 1 Scene 1

The Archbishop of Canterbury and the Bishop of Ely are worried about a Bill that will take power and riches from the Church. They talk about how they can stop this happening.

How, my lord, shall we resist it now?

The King is full of grace and fair regard.

The courses of his youth promised it not. The breath no sooner left his father's body but that his wildness seemed to die too.

And a true lover of the holy Church.

We are blessed in the change. But how now for this bill? Doth his majesty incline to it, or no?

He seems indifferent. I have made an offer to his majesty to give a greater sum than ever the **clergy** did to his **predecessors**.

How did this offer seem received?

With good acceptance, save that there was not time enough to hear.

The French ambassador **craved audience**, and the hour is come to give him hearing.

What was th'impediment that broke this off?

clergy – leaders of the church
predecessors – the kings before him
craved audience – asked to be seen

2

King Henry wants to make sure he has a right to the French throne. He asks for advice before he meets the French ambassador.

Shall we call in th'ambassador, my liege?

Not yet: we would be resolved before we hear him of some things of weight that task our thought, concerning us and France.

Unfold why the law Salic that they have in France should or should not bar us in our claim.

There is no bar but this – no woman shall succeed in Salic land. Yet the land Salic is in Germany, the Salic law was not devised for France.

May I with right and conscience make this claim?

Gracious lord, stand for your own, unwind **your bloody flag**.

Your brother kings and monarchs of the earth do all expect that you should rouse yourself, as did **the former lions of your blood**.

Call in the messengers sent from the Dauphin.

your bloody flag – your battle flag   **the former lions of your blood** – your ancestors

3

**Act 1
Scene 2**

The French ambassador brings an insulting message from the Dauphin!

Now are we well prepared to know the pleasure of our fair cousin Dauphin; for we hear your greeting is from him, not from the King.

Your highness lately sending into France did claim some certain dukedoms ...

... In answer of which claim the Prince our master says that you savour too much of your youth.

He therefore sends you, **meeter** for your spirit, this **tun** of treasure.

What treasure, uncle?

Tennis-balls, my liege.

meeter – more suitable   **tun** – barrel

| Act 1 Scene 2 | The King is angry with the present of tennis balls. He decides that he will make the Dauphin pay for this! He is now determined to fight France. |

King: We are glad the Dauphin is so pleasant with us.
His present and your pains we thank you for.
When we have matched our rackets to these balls
We will in France, by God's grace, play a set
Shall strike his father's crown into the hazard.
Tell him he hath made a match with such a **wrangler**

wrangler – opponent

That all the courts of France shall be disturbed
With chases. And we understand him well,
How he comes o'er us with our wilder days,
Not measuring what use we made of them.
But tell the Dauphin I will keep my state,
Be like a king and show my sail of greatness,
When I do rouse me in my throne of France.
I will rise there with so full a glory
That I will dazzle all the eyes of France,
Yea, strike the Dauphin blind to look on us.
And tell the pleasant Prince this mock of his
Hath turned his balls to **gun-stones**, and his soul

gun-stones – cannon balls

Shall stand sore charged for the wasteful vengeance
That shall fly with them; for many a thousand widows
Shall this his mock mock out of their dear husbands,
Mock mothers from their sons, mock castles down,
And some are yet ungotten and unborn
That shall have cause to curse the Dauphin's scorn.
But all this lies within the will of God,
To whom I do appeal, and in whose name
Tell you the Dauphin I am coming on
To venge me as I may, and to put forth
My rightful hand in a well-hallowed cause.
So get you hence in peace. And tell the Dauphin
His **jest** will savour but of shall wit

jest – joke

When thousands weep more than did laugh at it.

Think about it

Why do you think that the gift of tennis balls made the King determined to take revenge?

<table>
<tr><td>**Act 2**</td><td>The Chorus tells us that while people in England are preparing to go to fight in France, three traitors are ready to kill King Henry.</td></tr>
</table>

Chorus: Now all the youth of England are on fire,
And silken dalliance in the wardrobe lies.
Now thrive the armourers, and honour's thought
Reigns solely in the breast of every man.

The time to enjoy themselves is over

The French, advised by good intelligence
Of this most dreadful preparation,
Shake in their fear, and with pale policy
Seek to divert the English purposes
And three corrupted men,
One, Richard Earl of Cambridge, and the second,
Henry Lord Scroop of Masham, and the third,
Sir Thomas Grey, knight, of Northumberland,
Have, for the **gilt** of France, O guilt indeed! –
Confirmed conspiracy with fearful France,
And by their hands this grace of kings must die,
Ere he take shop for France.

gilt – gold/money

Act 2 Scene 1 — Before we meet the traitors who want to kill the King, we meet soldiers in a street in London who don't get on that well together!

What, are **Ancient** Pistol and you friends yet?

For my part, I care not. I say little.

I will bestow a breakfast to make you friends, and we'll be all three sworn brothers to France.

It is certain that Pistol is married to Nell Quickly, and certainly she did you wrong, for you were **troth-plight** to her.

I cannot tell. Things must be as they may.

Here comes Ancient Pistol and his wife.

How now, mine host Pistol?

Base tyke, by this hand I swear I scorn the term.

Good Lieutenant, good Corporal, **offer nothing here**.

Pish!

Iceland dog!

Ancient – Ensign (standard-bearer) **troth-plight** – engaged
Base tyke – mongrel dog **offer nothing here** – don't fight here

7

Think about it

Why is it important to show that soldiers on the same side don't always get on?

shog off – go away   **solus** – alone   **egregious** – outrageous
my master – Sir John Falstaff (a former friend of King Henry)

Act 2 Scene 2

The three traitors don't know that the King knows about their plans. Henry is about to deal with them but first he tricks them. He asks them what they would do to a person who spoke out against the King.

'Fore God, his grace is bold to trust these traitors.

They shall be apprehended by and by.

Now sits the wind fair, and we will abroad. Think you not that the powers we bear with us will cut their passage through the force of France?

No doubt, if each man do his best.

Never was monarch better feared and loved than is your majesty.

Those that were your father's enemies do serve you with hearts of duty and of zeal.

Uncle of Exeter, **enlarge** the man committed yesterday that railed against our person.

Let him be punished, sovereign.

O let us yet be merciful.

enlarge – set free

capital – serious   lose so much complexion – turn pale   quick – alive

<table>
<tr><td>**Act 2**
Scene 2</td><td>King Henry tells the traitors they will be executed. He goes on to tell his lords that they must head for France and trust in God.</td></tr>
</table>

King: God quit you in his mercy! Hear your sentence.
You have conspired against our royal person,
Joined with an enemy proclaimed and fixed,
And from his coffers
Received **the golden earnest of our death**;

payment for murdering King Henry

Wherein you would have sold your king to slaughter,
His princes and peers to servitude,
His subjects to oppression and contempt,
And his whole kingdom into desolation.
Touching our person we seek no revenge,
But we our kingdom's safety must so tender,
Whose ruin you have sought, that to her laws
We do deliver you. Get ye therefore hence,
Poor miserable wretches, to your death.

Now, lords, for France; the enterprise whereof
Shall be to you as us, like glorious.
We doubt not of a fair and lucky war,
Since God so graciously hath brought to light
This dangerous treason lurking in our way
To hinder our beginnings.
Then forth, dear countrymen. Let us deliver
Our **puissance** into the hand of God,

puissance – power

Putting it straight in expedition.
Cheerly to sea; the signs of war advance.
No king of England, if not king of France!

Think about it

Why is God mentioned three times in this speech?

Act 2 Scene 3

The knight, Sir John Falstaff, has died. He never got over the way King Henry no longer wanted to know him. He died with very few friends.

Falstaff is dead.

Would I were with him, either in heaven or in hell.

Nay, sure he's not in hell.

He parted just between twelve and one. I saw him fumble with the sheets and play with the **flowers**, and smile upon his fingers' ends. Now I, to comfort him, bid him he should not think of God – I hoped there was no need. He bade me put more clothes on his feet. I put my hand into the bed and all was cold as stone.

They say he cried out of **sack.**

Ay, that he did.

And of women.

Yes, he said once the devil would have him about women.

Shall we **shog**? The King will be gone from Southampton.

Let's away. My love, give me thy lips.

flowers – put on the bed to perfume the air   **sack** – sherry   **shog** – go

| Act 2 Scene 4 | The French king talks about the English king and his army. He is worried, but the Dauphin still does not think much of King Henry. |

Thus comes the English with full power upon us, and more than carefully it us concerns to answer royally in our defences. For England his approaches makes as fierce as waters to the sucking gulf.

Father, it is most meet we arm us 'gainst the foe. Let us do it with no show of fear than if we heard that England were busied with a Whitsun morris-dance.

For she is so idly kinged by a vain, giddy, shallow, humourous youth that fear attend her not.

You are too much mistaken in this king. You shall find **his vanities forespent**.

'Tis not so, my lord Constable, but it is no matter. 'Tis best to weigh the enemy more mighty than he seems.

Think we King Harry strong. Let us fear the native mightiness and fate of him.

his vanities forespent – he has changed since he became king

Exeter arrives to give the French king a message from King Henry who is already in France. He tells the French king to give up the throne or else . . .

Exeter: He bids you then resign
Your crown and kingdom indirectly held
From him the native and true challenger.

French King: Or else what follows?

Exeter: Bloody constraint; for if you hide the crown
Even in your heart, there will he rake for it.
Therefore in fierce tempest is he coming,
In thunder and in earthquake, like a **Jove**.
This is his claim, his threatening, and my message --
Unless the Dauphin be in presence here,
To whom expressly I bring greeting too.

Jove – The Roman god who could throw thunderbolts

Dauphin: For the Dauphin,
I stand here for him. What to him from England?

Exeter: Scorn and defiance, slight regard, contempt.
Thus says my king: an if your father's highness
Do not, in grant of all demands at large,
Sweeten the bitter mock you sent his majesty,
He'll call you to so hot an answer for it
That caves and **womby** vaultages of France
Shall chide your trespass and return your mock
In second accent of his ordinance.

womby – hollow

Dauphin: Say if my father render fair return
It is against my will, for I desire
Nothing but odds with England. To that end,
As matching to his youth and vanity,
I did present him with the Paris-balls.

Exeter: He'll make your Paris Louvre shake for it.
You'll find a difference
Between the promise of his greener days
And these he masters now.

Think about it

Do the French king and the Dauphin think differently about King Henry's threats?

Chorus: Thus with imagined wing our swift scene flies.
Suppose that you have seen
The well-appointed King at **Hampton** pier   **Hampton** – Southampton
Embark his royalty, and his brave fleet.
Play with your fancies, and in them behold
Upon the **hempen tackle** ship-boys climbing: **hempen tackle** – ropes
Hear the shrill whistle which doth order give
To sounds confused; behold the threaden sails.
Behold a city, for so appears this fleet majestical.
Work, work your thoughts, and therein see a siege.
Suppose th' ambassador from the French comes back,
Tells Harry that the King doth offer him
Katherine his daughter and with her, to dowry,
Some petty and unprofitable dukedoms.
The offer likes not; and the nimble gunner
With **linstock** now the devilish cannon touches,   **linstock** – a pole that holds a
And down goes all before them. Still be kind,   lighted fuse
And eke out our performance with your mind.

Act 3 Scene 1	The English army has attacked and been driven back from the walls of Harfleur. King Henry speaks to his soldiers to get them to attack again. He tells them to be proud that they are English and to show their bravery.	

King: Once more unto the breach, dear friends, once more,
Or close the wall up with our English dead.
In peace there's nothing so becomes a man
As modest stillness and humility;
But when the blast of war blows on our ears,
Then imitate the action of the tiger,
Stiffen the sinews, conjure up the blood,
Disguise fair nature with hard-favoured rage.
Then **lend the eye a terrible aspect**:   look fierce
Let it pry through the portage of the head
Like the brass cannon; let the brow o'erwhelm it
As fearfully as doth a galled rock
O'erhang and jutty his confounded base,
Swilled with the wild and wasteful ocean.
Now set the teeth, and stretch the nostril wide,
Hold hard the breath, and bend up every spirit
To his full height! On, on, you noble English,
Whose blood is fet from fathers of war-proof,
Fathers that like so many **Alexanders**   Alexander the Great
Have in these parts from morn till **even** fought,   **even** – evening
And sheathed their swords for lack of argument.
Dishonour not your mothers; now attest
That those whom you called fathers did beget you.
Be copy now to men of grosser blood   be an example
And teach them how to war. And you, good yeomen,
Whose limbs were made in England, show us here
The mettle of your pasture; let us swear   the quality of your upbringing
That you are worth your breeding – which I doubt not,
For there is none of you so mean and base
That hath not noble lustre in your eyes.
I see you stand like greyhounds in the slips,
Straining upon the start. The game's afoot.
Follow your spirit, and upon this charge
Cry, 'God for Harry! England, and Saint George!'

> **Think about it**
>
> Do you think this is an effective speech?
>
> Would it make a soldier feel proud and brave?

The soldiers talk about the war and how it is being fought.

On, on, on to the breach!

Pray thee, Corporal, stay, I have not a case of lives. **The humour of it is too hot**.

Would I were in an alehouse in London!

Up to the breach, you dogs!

As young as I am, I have observed these three swashers, but all three could not be a man to me.

Bardolph is **white-livered** and red-faced. Pistol hath a killing tongue and a quiet sword. For Nym, his few bad words are matched with as few good deeds.

They will steal anything, and call it purchase. They would have me as familiar with men's pockets.

I must leave them and seek some better service; their villainy goes against my weak stomach.

The humour ... too hot – It's too dangerous   **white-livered** – cowardly

mines – tunnels dug under the city's walls   falorous – valorous (brave)

Macmorris, will you vouchsafe me, look you, a few disputations with you, as partly touching or concerning the disciplines of the war?

It is no time to discourse, the town is **besieched**, and the trumpet calls us to the breach, and we talk and, **be Chrish** do nothing.

I think, look you, under your correction, there is not many of your nation ...

Who talks of my nation? I will cut off your head.

Gentlemen both, you mistake each other.

The town sounds a parley.

When there is better opportunity, look you, I will be so bold as to tell you I know the disciplines of war.

Think about it

Which soldiers came to war to steal and make money?

Which soldiers came to fight for king and country?

besieched – besieged   be Chrish – by Christ

| Act 3 Scene 3 | King Henry talks to the Governor of the French town of Harfleur. He tells him what will happen if they don't do as he says! They surrender! |

King: How yet resolves the Governor of the town?
This is the latest parle we will admit.
Therefore to our best mercy give yourselves.
If I begin the **battery** once again,
I will not leave the half-achieved Harfleur
Till in her ashes she lie buried.
The gates of mercy shall be all shut up
And the fleshed soldier, rough and hard of heart,
In liberty of bloody hand shall range
With conscience wide as hell, mowing like grass
Your fresh fair virgins, and your flowering infants.
Therefore, you men of Harfleur,
Take pity of your town and of your people
Whiles yet my soldiers are in my command,
Whiles yet the cool and temperate wind of grace
O'erblows the filthy and contagious clouds
Of heady murder, spoil and villainy.
If not, why, in a moment look to see
The blind and bloody soldier with foul hand
Defile the locks of your shrill-shrieking daughters,
Your fathers taken by the silver beards,
And their most reverend heads dashed to the walls,
Your naked infants spitted upon pikes,
Whiles the mad mothers with their howls confused
Do break the clouds, as did the wives of Jewry
At Herod's bloody-hunting slaughtermen.
What say you? Will you yield and this avoid?

Governor: We yield our town and lives to thy soft mercy.

King: Come, uncle Exeter,
Go you and enter Harfleur; there remain,
And fortify it strongly 'gainst the French.
Use mercy to them all. For us, dear uncle,
The winter coming on, and sickness growing
Upon our soldiers, we will retire to Calais.

battery – attack

Think about it

The English attack doesn't make the Governor surrender. Henry's words do!

Why is that?

Princess Katherine has a lesson in the English language from her servant, Alice.

Tu as été en Angleterre et tu parle bien le langage.

Un peu, madame.

Comment appelez-vous la main en anglais?

De hand.

Et les doigts?

De fingres.

J'ai gagné deux mots d'anglais vitement. Les ongles?

De nails.

Le bras?

De arm.

Le coude?

D'elbow.

Écoutez ... d'hand, de fingres, de nails, de arm, de bilbow ...

Tu as ... le langage – You have been in England and speak the language well.   **Un peu** – a little
Comment appelez-vous – what do you call ...   **Et les doigts?** – And the fingers?
J'ai gagné ... vitement – I've learnt two English words quickly.   **Écoutez** – listen

Comment appelez-vous le col? – What do you call the neck?
Je réciterai – I'll say it again   **coun** – gown
Allons-nous à dîner – let's go and eat

Act 3 Scene 5	The French nobles are amazed that the English are fighting so well. They feel ashamed of themselves. The French king sends his messenger to tell Henry to surrender now because the English army is weak and tired.

Constable: Where have they this **mettle**?   spirit of bravery
Is not their climate foggy, raw, and dull,
On whom, as in despite, the sun looks pale,
Killing their fruit with frowns? Can sodden water,
A **drench for sour-reined jades**, their **barley-broth**,   medicine for worn-out horses
Decoct their cold blood to such valiant heat?   **barley-broth** – beer
And shall our quick blood, spirited with wine,   **Decoct** – boil
Seem frosty? O, for honour of our land,
Let us not hang like roping icicles
Upon our houses' thatch, whiles a more frosty people
Sweat drops of gallant youth in our rich fields!

Dauphin: By faith and honour,
Our **madams** mock at us and plainly say   **madams** – wives
Our mettle is **bred out**, and they will give   **bred out** – exhausted
Their bodies to the lust of English youth,
To new-store France with bastard warriors.

French King: Where is Montjoy the Herald? Speed him hence:
Let him greet England with our sharp defiance.
Go down upon him, you have power enough,
And in a captive chariot into Rouen
Bring him our prisoner.

Constable: Sorry am I his numbers are so few,
His soldiers sick and famished in their march,
For I am sure when he shall see our army
He'll drop his heart into the sink of fear
And for achievement offer us his ransom.

French King: Haste on Montjoy,
And let him say to England that we will send
To know what willing ransom he will give.

> **Think about it**
>
> What words tell you that the French don't rate the English?
>
> Would you say they are worried?

The English army is on the march, fighting as it goes. Bardolph is to be hanged for stealing a religious picture. Pistol asks for him to be pardoned.

How now Fluellen? Come you from the bridge? Is the Duke of Exeter safe?

He is not, God be praised, any hurt in the world.

There is a lieutenant there I did see do gallant service. He is called Pistol.

I know him not.

Here is the man.

Captain, I thee beseech to do me favours. Bardolph, a soldier firm and sound of heart, hath stolen a pax and hanged must be.

Let not hemp his windpipe suffocate. Go speak – the Duke will hear thy voice.

If he were my brother, I would desire the Duke to put him to execution, for discipline ought to be used.

Die and be damned!

Why, this is an arrant rascal, I remember him now – a **bawd**, a **cutpurse**.

I'll assure you, he uttered as prave words at the bridge as you shall see in a summer's day.

'Tis a rogue that now and then goes to the wars to grace himself at his return into London under the form of a soldier.

If I find a hole in his coat, I will tell him my mind.

The King is coming.

What men have you lost, Fluellen?

Never a man, but one that is like to be executed for robbing a church.

One Bardolph, if your majesty know the man. His face is all **whelks and knobs** and his lips blows at his nose.

But his nose is executed, and his fire's out.

We would have all such offenders so cut off; we give express charge that nothing be **compelled** from the villages, nothing taken but paid for.

bawd – pimp   **cutpurse** – thief   **If I find … coat** – If I find he's pretending
all whelks and knobs – all lumps and sores   **compelled** – forced

Act 3 Scene 6	Montjoy, the French herald (messenger), comes to threaten King Henry. The King sends him back, saying that they will continue to fight, even though the army is weak.	

Montjoy: Thus says my King: 'Say thou to Harry of England, though we seemed dead, we did but sleep. Advantage is a better soldier than rashness. Tell him we could have rebuked him at Harfleur, but that we thought not good to bruise an injury till it were full ripe. England shall repent his folly, see his weakness, and admire our sufferance. Bid him therefore, consider of his ransom.'

King: Turn thee back,
And tell thy King I do not seek him now,
But could be willing to march on to Calais
Without impeachment; for, to say the **sooth**,   **sooth** – truth
Though 'tis no wisdom to confess so much,
My people are with sickness much enfeebled,
My numbers lessened, and those few I have
Almost no better than so many French;
Who when they were in health, I tell thee, herald,
I thought upon one pair of English legs
Did march three Frenchmen.
Go, therefore, tell thy master here I am
My ransom is **this frail and worthless trunk**,   my body
My army but a weak and sickly guard.
Yet, God before, tell him we will come on,
Though France himself and such another neighbour,
Stand in our way.
We would not seek a battle as we are,
Nor as we are, we say we will not shun it.
So tell your master.   [*Montjoy leaves.*]

Gloucester: I hope they will not come upon us now.

King: We are in God's hand, brother, not in theirs.

Think about it

Does the King appear to be honest and honourable here?

The French nobles are eager to get on with the fighting. They talk about their armour and horses and the way they will fight. When the Dauphin leaves, they talk about him too.

I have the best armour of the world. Would it were day!

You have an excellent armour; but let my horse have his due.

My lord of Orleans and my lord High Constable, you talk of horse and armour?

You are as well provided of both as any prince in the world.

What a long night this is!

My lord Constable, the armour that I saw in your tent tonight – are those stars or suns upon it?

Stars, my lord.

Some of them **will fall** tomorrow, I hope.

And yet my sky shall not want.

I will trot tomorrow a mile and my way shall be paved with English faces. 'Tis midnight; I'll go arm myself.

will fall – will be knocked off in the battle

27

Act 3 Scene 7	The French nobles insult King Henry and his army. They boast about how many Englishmen they will kill or capture.	

Constable: Would it were day! Alas, poor Harry of England! He longs not for the dawning as we do.

Orleans: What a wretched and peevish fellow is this King of England, to mope with his fat-brained followers so far out of his knowledge!

Constable: If the English **had any apprehension** they would run away.

knew what was going to happen to them

Orleans: That they lack, for if their heads had any intellectual armour they could never wear such heavy headpieces.

their skulls are so thick, there is no room for brains

Rambures: That island of England breeds very valiant creatures: Their **mastiffs** are of unmatchable courage.

a breed of dog

Orleans: Foolish curs, that run winking into the mouth of a Russian bear, and have their heads crushed like rotten apples. You may as well say that's a valiant flea that dare eat his breakfast on the lip of a lion.

Constable: Just, just; and the men do sympathize with the mastiffs in robustious and rough coming on, leaving their wits with their wives. And then give them great meals of beef and iron and steel, they will eat like wolves, and fight like devils.

Orleans: Ay, but these English **are shrewdly out of** beef.

are short of

Constable: Then shall we find tomorrow they have only stomachs to eat and none to fight. Now is it time to arm. Come, shall we about it?

Orleans: It is now two o'clock; but, let me see, by ten we shall have each a hundred Englishmen.

Think about it

Why do the French need to boast and insult the English?

<table>
<tr><td>

Act 4

</td><td>

The Chorus describes the different moods of the French and English armies the night before the battle. King Henry walks through his camp talking to his soldiers, telling them to be brave.

</td></tr>
</table>

Chorus: From camp to camp through the foul womb of night
The hum of either army stilly sounds,
That the fixed sentinels almost receive   *The sentries are almost close*
The secret whispers of each other's watch.   *enough to hear each other*
Proud of their numbers and secure in soul,
The confident and over-lusty French
Do the low-rated English **play at dice**,   *gambling the English prisoners they*
And chide the cripple tardy-gaited night   *expect to capture*
Who like a foul and ugly witch doth limp
So tediously away. The poor condemned English,
Like sacrifices, by their watchful fires
Sit patiently and **inly ruminate**   *think to themselves*
The morning's danger. O now, who will behold
The royal captain of this ruined band
Walking from watch to watch, from tent to tent,
For forth he goes and visits all his host,
Bids them good morrow with a modest smile,
And calls them brothers, friends and countrymen.
Every wretch, pining and pale before,
Beholding him plucks comfort from his looks.
His liberal eye doth give to every one,
Thawing cold fear, that **mean and gentle all**   *ordinary men and nobles*
Behold, as may unworthiness define,
A little touch of Harry in the night.

Think about it

Who do you think seem more confident – the French or the English?

Act 4 Scene 1

King Henry knows his army is in great danger. He borrows a cloak and walks through the camp. He meets with some soldiers who don't recognise him.

Qui va la?

A friend.

Art thou officer, or art thou base, common and popular?

I am a **gentleman of a company**, what are you?

As good a gentleman as the emperor. What is thy name.

Harry le Roy.

A Cornish name. Art thou of Cornish crew?

No, I am a Welshman.

Know'st thou Fluellen? Tell him I'll knock his leek about his pate upon Saint Davy's day.

Do not wear your dagger in your cap that day, lest he knock that about yours.

Qui va la? – Who goes there?   **gentleman of a company** – a gentleman but not an officer

31

estate – position   meet – right

Act 4 Scene 1	Williams and the King discuss whether a king is to blame for the crimes of the people who serve him.

Williams: But if the cause be not good, the King himself hath a heavy reckoning to make when all those legs and arms and heads chopped off in a battle shall join together at the latter day and cry all 'We died at such a place', some swearing, some crying for a surgeon, some upon their wives left poor behind them, some upon the debts they owe, some upon their children rawly left. I am afeard there are few die well that die in a battle, for how can they charitably dispose of anything when blood is their argument? Now if these men do not die well it will be a black matter for the King, that led them to it, who to disobey were against all proportion of subjection.

King: So if a son that is by his father sent about merchandise do sinfully miscarry upon the sea, the imputation of his wickedness, by your rule, should be imposed upon his father that sent him; or if a servant, under his master's command transporting a sum of money, be assailed by robbers and die in many irreconciled iniquities, you may call the business of the master the author of the servant's damnation. But this is not so: the King is not bound to answer the particular endings of his soldiers, the father of his son, nor the master of his servant; for they purpose not their death when they purpose their services. Besides, there is no king, be his cause never so spotless, if it come to the arbitrement of swords, can try it out with all unspotted soldiers. Some have on them the guilt of premeditated and contrived murder, some of beguiling virgins with the broken seals of perjury, some, making the wars their **bulwark**, that have before gored the gentle bosom of peace with pillage and robbery. Now if these men have defeated the law and outrun native punishment, though they can outstrip men, they have no wings to fly from God. Every subject's duty is the King's, but every subject's soul is his own. Therefore should every soldier in the wars do as every sick man in his bed, wash every mote out of his conscience.

bulwark – security

Think about it

Can you find the evidence that Williams and the King are talking about slightly different things?

Williams and the King continue to discuss whether the King is to be trusted. Williams still doesn't know he is talking to the King himself. They agree to swap gloves and wear them in their caps. If they live and meet again, they will challenge each other.

'Tis certain, every man that dies ill, the ill upon his own head – the King is not to answer for it.

I do not desire he should answer for me, and yet I determine to fight lustily for him.

I myself heard the King say he would not be ransomed.

He said so to make us fight cheerfully, but when our throats are cut he may be ransomed, and we ne'er the wiser.

If I live to see it, I will never trust his word again.

'Tis a foolish saying.

I should be angry with you, if this time were convenient.

I embrace it – I agree   enow – enough

<table>
<tr><td>Act 4
Scene 1</td><td>Henry is alone. He begins to think about the problems and responsibilities of being the King. He thinks of the lives of the common men and then thinks about his own.</td><td></td></tr>
</table>

King: Upon the King! 'Let us our lives, our souls,
Our debts, our careful wives,
Our children and our sins lay on the King!'
We must bear all. O hard condition,
Twin-born with greatness, subject to the breath
Of every fool, whose sense no more can feel
But his own wringing!
I am a king, and I know
'Tis not the balm, the sceptre and the ball,
The sword, the mace, the crown imperial,
The intertissued robe of gold and pearl,
The farced title running 'fore the king,
The throne he sits on, nor the tide of pomp
That beats upon the high shore of this world,
No, not all these, thrice-gorgeous ceremony,
Not all these, laid in bed majestical,
Can sleep so soundly as the wretched slave,
Who with a body filled and vacant mind
Gets him to rest, crammed with distressful bread:
Never sees horrid night, the child of hell,
But like a lackey from the rise to set
Sweats in the eye of **Phoebus**, and all night
Sleeps in **Elysium**. Such a wretch
Had the fore-hand and vantage of a king.

O God of battles, steel my soldiers' hearts;
Possess them not with fear. Take from them now
The sense of reckoning, if th'opposed numbers
Pluck their hearts from them.

Phoebus – the sun god
Elysium – Paradise
(i.e. without any troubles)

Think about it

What words show that the King might not be confident?

What do you think he dreams about?

Act 4 Scene 2

It is morning and the French are ready to fight. One of them has seen the English army. He says that they look weak and will be beaten easily.

The sun doth gild our armour: up my lords!

The English are **embattled**, you French peers.

To horse, you gallant princes, straight to horse! Let the trumpet sound. Our approach shall so much dare the field that England shall couch down in fear and yield.

The horsemen sit like fixed candlesticks, their poor **jades** lob down their heads. The knavish crows fly o'er them all, impatient for their hour.

They have said their prayers and they **stay** for death. To the field!

embattled – in position   **jades** – worn out horses   **stay** – wait

<table>
<tr><td>

**Act 4
Scene 3**

</td><td>

King Henry tells his men they should be proud to fight. Any who want to leave, he tells them, can go! Those who fight bravely and live will be able to tell those who did not fight, what a wonderful time it was.

</td></tr>
</table>

Westmorland: O that we now had here
But one ten thousand of those men in England
That do no work today!

King: No, my fair cousin:
If we are marked to die, we are enough.
O do not wish one more!
Rather proclaim it, Westmorland, through my host,
That he which hath no stomach to this fight,
Let him depart; his passport shall be made
And **crowns for convoy** put into his purse.   money to pay for his journey home
We would not die in that man's company
That fears his fellowship to die with us.
This day is called the feast of Crispian.   25th October
He that outlives this day and comes safe home
Will stand a-tiptoe when this day is named
And rouse him at the name of Crispian.
He that shall see this day and live old age
Will yearly on the vigil feast his neighbours,
And say 'Tomorrow is Saint Crispian.'
Then will he strip his sleeve and show his scars,
And say 'These wounds I had on Crispin's Day.'
Old men forget; yet all shall be forgot
But he'll remember, with advantages,
What feats he did that day.
This story shall the good man teach his son,
And Crispin Crispian shall ne'er go by
But in it we shall be remembered.
We few, we happy few, we band of brothers,
For he today who sheds his blood with me
Shall be my brother.
And gentlemen in England now abed
Shall think themselves accursed they were not here,
And hold their manhoods cheap whiles any speaks
That fought with us upon Saint Crispin's Day.

Think about it

Do you think the King is right? Will his soldiers boast about the battle in the future?

The King's men are ready to fight now that he has spoken to them. The French herald comes again to discuss the terms of surrender. Henry tells him that he will never surrender!

The French are bravely **in their battles set**, and will with all expedience charge on us.

All things are ready.

Thou dost not wish more help from England, **coz**?

You and I alone could fight this royal battle.

Once more I come to know of thee, King Harry, if for thy ransom thou wilt now compound before thy most assured overthrow.

Who hath sent thee now?

The Constable of France.

I pray thee bear my former answer back:
Bid them **achieve** me and then sell my bones.
Tell the Constable
We are but **warriors for the working-day**.
And time hath worn us into slovenry.
But by the mass, our hearts are in the trim.
Come no more for ransom, gentle herald.
They shall have none, I swear, but these my joints.

in their battles set – in position   **coz** – cousin   **achieve** – capture
warriors for the working-day – ordinary soldiers with no fine clothes

Act 4 Scene 4

Pistol has caught a French solider but decides that he will let him go if the soldier pays him. The Boy thinks Pistol is no good. He goes off to guard the equipment at the English camp.

Yield cur! What is thy name?

O Seigneur Dieu!

Signieur Dew, thou diest on point of **fox**, except thou do give to me ransom.

Ayez pitié de moi!

I will have forty moys, or I will fetch thy **rim** out at thy throat in drops of crimson blood.

Est-il impossible d'échapper la force de ton bras?

Brass, cur? Offer'st me brass?

O Seigneur Dieu! – O Lord God!   **fox** – sword   **Ayez pitié de moi!** – Have pity on me!
rim – stomach lining   **Est-il ... bras?** – Is it impossible to escape the strength of your arm?

Suivez-vous le grand capitaine – Follow the great captain.

Act 4 Scene 5

The French cannot believe that their attack has failed and their army is retreating. Some of the nobles say that they will fight and die rather than suffer the shame of defeat.

O Seigneur! Le jour est perdu, tout est perdu!

All our ranks are broke.

Be these the wretches that we played at dice for?

Is this the King we sent to for his ransom?

Disorder, that hath spoiled us, friend us now.

We are enough yet living in the field to smother up the English in our throngs if any order might be thought upon.

The devil take order now! I'll to the throng. Let life be short, else shame will be too long.

O Seigneur ... est perdu! – O God! The day is lost, all is lost!

44

They find out that the French have killed the boys guarding the equipment.

Kill the poys and the luggage!

'Tis certain there's not a boy left alive.

The cowardly rascals that ran from the battle ha' done this slaughter. They have burned and carried away all that was in the King's tent, wherefore the King hath caused every soldier to cut his prisoner's throat. O, 'tis a gallant king!

Ay, he was porn at Monmouth. What call you the town's name where Alexander the Pig was born?

Alexander the Great.

Is not pig great?

I think Alexander the Great was born in Macedon.

Macedon and Monmouth is both alike. There is a river in Macedon and there is also moreover a river at Monmouth.

If you mark Alexander's life well, Harry of Monmouth's life is come after it well. There's good men porn at Monmouth.

<table>
<tr><td>

**Act 4
Scene 7**

</td><td>

King Henry is mad at the French, but he finds out that the English have won the battle. He lets the French look for their dead, to bury them. He calls the battle – Agincourt, after the nearby castle.

</td></tr>
</table>

King: I was not angry since I came to France
Until this instant. Take a trumpet, herald;
Ride thou unto the horsemen on yon hill.
If they will fight with us bid them come down,
Or *void* the field: they do offend our sight.

void – leave

Besides, we'll cut the throats of those we have,
and not a man of them that we shall take
Shall taste our mercy. Go and tell them so.

Exeter: Here comes the herald of the French.

[*Enter* Montjoy]

King: Com'st thou again for ransom?

Montjoy: No great King:
I come to thee for **charitable licence**
That we may wander o'er this bloody field
To look our dead and then to bury them;
To sort our nobles from our common men.

permission

King: I tell thee truly, herald,
I know not if the day be ours or no,
For yet a many of your horsemen peer
And gallop o'er the field.

Montjoy: The day is yours.

King: Praised be God, and not our strength for it!
What is this castle called that stands hard by?

Montjoy: They call it Agincourt.

King: Then call we this the field of Agincourt,
Fought on the day of Crispin Crispian.

Think about it

Is King Henry a merciful king?

plows – blows   in change – in exchange

Act 4 Scene 8	The King sorts out the trouble. He finds out how many men have lost their lives and orders that prayers be said for them. He plans to go home to England.

King: Give me thy glove, soldier. Look, here is the fellow of it. 'Twas I indeed thou promis'd to strike.

Williams: All offences, my lord, come from the heart: never came any from mine that might offend your majesty.

King: It was our self thou didst abuse.

Williams: Your majesty came not like yourself: you appeared to me but as a common man. I beseech your highness pardon me.

King: Here uncle Exeter, fill this glove with *crowns*
And give it to this fellow. Keep it, fellow,
And wear it for an honour in thy cap
Till I do challenge it. Give him the crowns:
And Captain, you must needs be friends with him.

crowns – money

Fluellen: By this day and this light, the fellow has mettle enough in his belly. Hold, there is twelve pence for you, and keep you out of **prawls**, **prabbles** and quarrels.

brawls, small arguments

Williams: I will none of your money.

Fluellen: It is with a good will. I can tell you, it will serve you to mend your shoes.

King: Now herald, are the dead numbered?
This note doth tell me of ten thousand French
That in the field lie slain.
Where is the number of our English dead?
But five and twenty. O God, thy arm was here!

Think about it

What have you got to say about the numbers dead?

Would an audience notice this and say anything?

native garb – like an Englishman   **patches** – dressings/bandages

The French King is going to look at Henry's demands, now that the English have won the war. King Henry wants to marry Princess Katherine, so he tries to court her.

Peace to this meeting.

Right joyous are we to behold your face, most worthy brother of England.

So happy be the issue of this good day.

You must buy peace will full accord to all our just demands.

The King hath heard them, to the which as yet there is no answer made.

I have o'erglanced the articles. Pleaseth your grace to appoint some of your council to sit with us once more to re-survey them.

We shall. Will you, fair sister, go with the princes, or stay here?

I will go with them.

Yet leave Katherine here with us.

| Act 5 Scene 2 | King Henry wants to tell Katherine that he loves her. He says he is not very good with words, but he tries his best. |

King: Kate, I cannot look greenly, nor gasp out my eloquence, nor I have no cunning in protestation, only downright oaths, which I never use till urged, nor never break for urging. If thou canst love a fellow of this temper, Kate, whose face is not worth sunburning, that never looks in his glass for love of anything he sees there, let thine eye be thy cook. I speak to thee plain soldier. If thou canst love me for this, take me; if not by the Lord, no; yet I love thee too. And while thou liv'st, dear Kate, take a fellow of plain and uncoined constancy; for he perforce must do thee right, because he hath not the gift to woo in other places. A black beard will turn white, a curled **pate** will grow bald, a fair face will wither; but a good heart, Kate, is the sun and the moon – or rather the sun and not the moon, for it shines bright and never changes but keeps his course truly. If thou would have such a one, take me: and take me, take a soldier; take a soldier take a king. And what say'st thou then to my love? Speak, my fair, and fairly, I pray thee.

pate – head

Katherine: Is it possible dat I sould love the enemy of France?

King: No, it is not possible you should love the enemy of France, Kate: but in loving me you should love the friend of France; for I love France so well that I will not part with a village of it – I will have it all mine: and Kate, when France is mine, and I am yours, then yours is France and you are mine.

Think about it

Katherine asks an awkward question.

What do you think of the King's reply?

Is he clever or not?

King Henry succeeds in getting Katherine to marry him.

When I come to woo ladies I fright them. But in faith, Kate, the elder I wax the better I shall appear. Old age can do no more spoil upon my face. Tell me, will you have me?

Dat is as it sall please **le roi mon père**.

It will please him well, Kate.

Den it sall also content me.

Upon that I kiss your hand and I call you my Queen.

Les dames et les demoiselles pour être baisées devant leur noces, il n'est pas la coutume de France.

O Kate, nice customs curtsey to great kings. We are the makers of manners, Kate.

le roi mon père – the King my father   **Les dames ... de France** – It's not the custom in France, for ladies and young ladies to be kissed before their wedding day.

| **Act 5 Scene 2** | King Henry and the French King reach agreement. Katherine is to marry Henry. Things have turned out well for the English King. |

French King: We have consented to all terms of reason.

King: Is't so, my lords of England?

Westmorland: The King hath granted every article:
His daughter first, and in the sequel all,
According to their firm proposed natures

King: I pray you then, give me your daughter.

French King: Take her, fair son and from her blood raise
up issue to me, that the contending kingdoms
Of France and England, whose very shores look pale
With envy of each other's happiness,
May cease their hatred, and this dear conjunction
Plant neighbourhood and Christian-like accord
In their sweet bosoms, that never war advance
His bleeding sword 'twixt England and Fair France.

King: Now welcome, Kate and bear me witness all
That here I kiss her as my sovereign queen.

Queen Isabel: God, the best maker of all marriages,
Combine your hearts in one, your realms in one!
As man and wife, being two, are one in love,
So be there 'twixt your kingdoms such a **spousal**
That never may ill office, or fell jealousy,
Which troubles oft the bed of blessed marriage,
Thrust in between the paction of these kingdoms
To make divorce of their incorporate league;
That England may as French, French Englishmen,
Receive each other. God speak this 'Amen'!

spousal – marriage

King: Prepare we for our marriage; on which day,
My lord of Burgundy we'll take our oath
And the peers', for surety of our leagues.
Then shall I swear to Kate, and you to me,
And may our oaths well kept and prosperous be!

> **Think about it**
>
> This looks like a happy ending. Has the play ended happily for everbody in it?

The Chorus tells us a bit more about King Henry and his son now that we have seen the play.

He goes on to tell us that France was lost after Henry the Fifth died.

Chorus: Thus far, with rough and all-unable pen,
Our bending author hath pursued the story,
In little room confining mighty men,
Mangled by starts the full course of their glory.
Small time, but in that small most greatly lived
This star of England. Fortune made his sword
By which the world's best garden he achieved,
And of it left his son imperial lord.
Henry the Sixth, in infant bands crowned King
Of France and England, did this king succeed,
Whose state so many had the managing
That they lost France and made his England bleed,
Which oft our stage hath shown; and for their sake
In your fair minds let this acceptance take.

Think about it

What reason does the Chorus give for England losing France under Henry the Sixth?

Does that affect the way we think about this War now?